A VIEW FROM THE BRIDGE

PHOTOGRAPHY: JOHN INGLEDEW   TEXT: GRAHAM WRAY

More Than Ninety Minutes Publishing Company

ACKNOWLEDGMENTS

Thanks to Adrian Wells, Martin Wells,
Pat Nevin, James Edwards, Tom Sayer,
Dave Hendley, Jake Whiteley,
Paul Hawksbee, Leigh Davies, Dick Jewell,
Arthur Miller, Neil Onslow, Joe Boylan,
Viresh Chopra, Ian Middleton,
Nick Clabham, Adrian Ensor,
Red Saunders and Dermot Goulding.

For EJ, D, O and DR.

See you at The Bridge.

Copyright © 1998
More Than Ninty Minutes Publishing Co.

All rights reserved. No part of this publication may be reproduced, stored in a retrieval system or transmitted in any form or by any means, electronic, mechanical, photocopying, recording or otherwise without the prior written permission of the publishers.

The views expressed in this book are not necessarily those of the publisher.

Published by:
More Than Ninety Minutes Publishing Co.
Manor Barn, Poynings Road, Poynings,
Brighton, East Sussex BN45 7AG
Telephone: 01273 857388

Designed and printed by:
Detail Print,
Manor Barn, Poynings Road, Poynings,
Brighton, East Sussex BN45 7AG.
Telephone: 01273 857449

ISBN - 0 9531214 1 0

FOREWORD by Pat Nevin

This book is aimed at fans, football fans in general, Chelsea fans in particular. Portrayed here are many poignant personal moments and scenes easily recognisable to the real 'owners' of the football club - the fans. These are the people who give a club its true character and identity. True fans will look at these photographs and immediately recall their own very personal individual feelings and experiences related to them. Of course because they are the club, this work is in effect as much a homage to them as to anyone.

Okay, so I'm only a player, but I feel part of it too. For a long time I flatter myself that I was a loyal fan as well as a player. I used to walk to the games from my flat in Earls Court and the next season when I moved to Pimlico I frequently got the Number 11 bus to the games. This is why I can empathise with so many of the images here. For a couple of years I arrived as a fan, before walking onto the park instead of into the Shed.

It is interesting to see someone else's perspective on a place you know so well, especially if he is a talented photographer with an obvious feeling for his subject. Many of the photographs are stories in themselves and like the best of their art, they are more eloquent than a thousand words.

I miss Stamford Bridge and Chelsea, but TV footage of games has rarely moved me. However, some of these pictures did. I was happy that it conjured many memories but more moved by the emotions it disturbed in me. There was happiness, sadness, joy, regret and well, just all the emotions you would expect to have about something you loved.

INTRODUCTION by James Edwards - Editor of the Chelsea Independent

This is a book about fans of Chelsea Football Club.

Many football books focus on strikers scoring, defenders tackling, keepers saving and silverware being lifted, this book is different. A View From The Bridge is a photographic history devoted entirely to the fans.

The history of a football club is as dependent on its supporters as it is on the scorelines and cup runs. Where history books record league positions, fans remember inflatable bananas. Where Rothmans list captains and transfer prices - the Chelsea faithful recall celery. It is football fans who form the culture of a club.

At the start of the 15 years recorded in this book the team was playing its football in the old second division having just avoided the drop to the third. The stadium, though much loved, was crumbling with large sections of the terraces fenced off because they were unsafe. The changes since then have been profound - what has not changed in all that time is the singular dedication of the fans.

What you may see in this book is yourself. If you have been a regular at Stamford Bridge you will be able to point to the terracing where you stood and say "I was there". And yes, you really did look like that!

This is not just an exercise in nostalgia, it serves as a useful reminder to all football fans of where we have just come from and illustrates the path of a loyalty that has lasted, it will probably last longer than your marriage or your mortgage.

Though the team of 1998 play attractive football, some of those that preceded them definitely did not, but a football club cannot be judged solely by the team they send out onto the pitch or by their board of directors or manager because these things change . What remains are the fans, whether lads in cardigans with number two haircuts or women with Prada handbags, what comes across in these photographs is the creation of the culture that plays in blue on a Saturday afternoon. We represent the family of Chelsea Football Club and this is our family album.

The distant glow of floodlights - always a sight to set fans' hearts racing. Particularly as kick-off looms and, as here, you're still twenty sodding minutes away.

The tension of an April 1982 relegation battle against Oldham takes its toll. Hands fidget in Wrangler pockets, teeth are gritted, No.6 are exhaled and more worryingly, programmes chewed.

Life in the Shed during the early '80s. Chelsea struggling at the foot of the Second Division, Geoff Hurst at the helm and only a dog turd for company. Guess that's why they call them the Blues.

A young fan mysteriously takes to hiding his lustrous Chelsea silk scarf. Possibly for fear of overstating things. Much envied at the time, the milk bottle sew-on badge currently possesses a market value in excess of £5,000. Probably.

Before the days when celebrities flocked to the Bridge, Chelsea relied on faithful, dyed-in-the-wool supporters from the local community. Forget painted faces, monikered shirts and the attentions of David Mellor - in May 1983, allegiance could be signified by nothing more outlandish than a pair of Sta-pressed slacks and a woollen scarf bearing half a ton of scrap metal.

Captured in the Fulham Road, this particular fan's body language suggests a surly indifference to the photographer's chirpy banter. Or perhaps it's merely a pose designed to maximise exposure of his to-die-for Casio watch.

Who said all early 1980s kits were naff? Compared to today's yellow and blue monstrosity, the Chelsea shirt of 1983 (obligatory pin-stripes aside) has proved to be a near classic. Unfortunately our friend on the left chose to ignore the golden rule that decreed that while white socks may be acceptable on the field of play, on the Fulham Road they're an absolute no-no.

True Blue in chunky knitwear horror! And even a glittering 1-1 draw with Rotherham fails to lift the depression.

Hard to believe that this ramshackle combination of timber, concrete and corrugated iron could have once been regarded as a bastion of invincibility. But throughout the 1970s and early '80s, 'the Shed' was revered by its inhabitants who took pride in the fear and loathing that it inspired in opposing fans. Taken in May 1984, the portrait captures the entrance to the Shed prior to the derby game against Fulham. Ironic then, that the home of Chelsea's most fervent fans has now been replaced by a different hard core - the foundations of a five star hotel. So where Chelsea's top boys once clashed with the opposition, city top boys now tangle with nothing more menacing than a Corby trouser press. Such is football in the late '90s.

The height of the casual era heralds the arrival of the Lacoste emblem. A closer inspection of the massed ranks on this terrace is a must for two reasons: one, it finally reveals the identity of the bloke who always starts the chanting; and two, it offers an unrivalled opportunity to play 'spot the female'.

April 1984, and while Chelsea's kit took a turn for the worse (hooped shirts!), the team's fortunes refused to follow suit. A 5-0 thumping of Leeds ensured promotion back to the First Division - the crowd rising as one to milk the moment. Save for one apparently Headingly born copper, caught making briskly for the exit.

Promotion clinched and the joyous thousands salute victorious manager John Neal, clearly visible 520th from the left.

Chelsea's return to the top flight is all too much for one high spirited pitch invader. Fortunately a sympathetic policeman is on hand to impart some fatherly advice. Namely that if you're going to threaten the Leeds fans with a good kicking it's advisable to ensure you've put your shoes on first.

It's not exactly every day you crush your arch enemies and steamroller your way back into the big time. So what are the odds on the wiry arm of the law clearing the pitch and quelling the party spirit . . .?

. . . about as slim, it would appear, as Mickey Droy.

While this Chelsea scratchcard seller's idea for a similar product later caught on nationally, sadly his handy programme storage system failed to catch the public's imagination in quite the same way.

An uneventful afternoon judging by some of the mournful expressions leaving via the steps from the West Stand. Although not for one bloke (third to the right of the lamppost, three rows from the top) who can't quite believe he's rubbing shoulders with Limahl from Kajagoogoo.

Fingers to the fore as Chelsea score another against Spurs. Meanwhile one Spurs fan (bottom left) has seen enough and mistakenly believes she can sneak out without being seen.

With victory assured, the air turns blue.

Somehow 'We'll keep the yellow banana flying high' just doesn't have the same ring to it. April 1989 - and the man responsible for the impending inflatable craze is brought to book.

The warm, homely, welcoming atmosphere of the Shed terrace, 1990.

A lone fan finds a unique vantage point...

28

... though why anyone would actually want to climb 30ft in order to get a better view of a rusting corrugated roof remains a mystery. More riveting than Chelsea's midfield at the time, presumably.

April 1989 and following the obligatory victory over Leeds (this time only 1- 0), the Blues are promoted as Champions of Barclays Division 2. Who'd have thought things could get any better?

Die-hards pack the Shed End steps, the back row displaying admirable balance on the crush barriers. Alas the sight of all that mysteriously entertaining football is evidently too much for one confused QPR fan who beats an early retreat down the steps.

A stroll up Wembley Way and three Chelsea fans experience first hand that famous tingling sensation in the loins. Such was the allure of Zenith Data Systems Finals in 1990.

Who needs Sky's dancing girls when you've got a stick of celery for pre-match entertainment. Chelsea fans rightfully claimed copyright on the bizarre 'celery' song long before it was taken up by rival fans. On this occasion, bemused Wembley officials confiscated thousands of celery sticks, fearing that they would be used as weapons. Thus saving Middlesbrough fans the ignominy of being 'ran' by a particularly menacing Waldorf salad.

The unbridled joy that only a Zenith Data Systems Final and a worm burger can provide. Back in the days when, judging by our two friends, CJD appeared to have an incubatory period of seven and a half seconds.

Chelsea take to the field for the 1990 Zenith Data Systems Final against Boro. A Mickey Mouse Cup? Try telling that to the 76,369 who saw Chelsea scoop the silverware thanks to a goal from Tony Dorigo.

Difficult to know what's more unsettling - a latecomer squeezing past you or his pre-match fare in your face

Packed terraces, clear skies and an abundance of shirtsleeves and optimism. It just has to be the opening day of the season. In August 1990, a 2-1 defeat of Derby gave even Stan Collymore (far left) cause to celebrate. Though come May, Chelsea duly returned to mid-table obscurity.

The creche under the East Stand still provides all manner of distractions for 90 minutes. Toys, games and as seen here in the background, even painting lessons.

A 1990 graduate from said Chelsea Creche School of Art gets his first showing in the Fulham back streets.

A gloomy December afternoon in 1990, a humdrum league fixture against Spurs, yet still the Bridge managed to generate it's familiar wall of harsh, discordant noise. Though why this West Stand regular has risen jubilantly to his feet with Spurs in possession on the halfway line is anyone's guess. Perhaps he was celebrating the fact he only had to pay seven quid for his seat.

Even in 1990, a ticket for Old Trafford was an item to behold. So perhaps the fiercely protective are-you-lookin'-at-my-ticket pose is understandable. On this particular November afternoon, an impressive 3-2 Chelsea victory set the tone for the rest of the decade - the Blues doing more than most to continually provide regulars at the Theatre of Dreams with the stuff of nightmares.

In 1990, the players tunnel provided a more gladitorial entrance to the pitch, one that almost demanded contenders sprint out in battle formation. Now sadly demolished, today's players have to make do with ambling out beneath a less than inspiring B&Q style canopy. A shambolic style of entrance that doesn't so much make the players resemble fearsome warriors, more like irritable housewives searching for the taramasalata in Tesco's.

The palatial splendour of the home dressing room, 1990. Athlete's foot anyone?

Not an early prototype of the National Lottery's Guinevere machine but in fact the East Stand seats. How many times has the ground echoed to the ominous clacking of these upturned beauties, ten minutes before the end of yet another listless performance?

The souvenir shop window on Fulham Broadway provides a fitting reflection of Chelsea's 1991 form. As the promo poster implies, the six best matches video featured the 3-0 Rumbelows Cup quarter final replay victory at Spurs. Six times.

Chelsea apprentices clear snow from the Shed terraces in February 1991. That youngster on the right, flashing his thermal Umbro gloves, wouldn't be a teenage Kevin Hitchcock by any chance? Or that scamp on the left, a fully grown Mark Stein? Thought not.

"Someone's sitting there mate . . ."
No anthology of Stamford Bridge would be complete without a Chelsea pensioner. Puffing quietly on his pipe, this veteran sits and quietly ponders the key issues of the day. Like 'where have all my mates legged it to?' Gone to sort the Tottenham boys, presumably.

Not what you could call aesthetically pleasing but nonetheless sturdy, imposing and reliably motionless whatever the conditions. A bit like Doug Rougvie in his prime.

Club Megastores? Pah! In 1991, pennants and team photos could be purchased from the Chelsea . . . ahem . . . souvenir hut. Not much call for Chelsea dressing gowns, fine wines and Harley-Davidsons in those days.

The local derby against QPR is always a crowd puller. No surprises then that for the 1991 fixture it was standing room only at the Shed's 'Bovril Gate'. Was this the beginning of corporate sponsorship?

You only get this sort of self-satisfied look when you've either pissed in the anorak pocket of the bloke in front, or your side is busy pissing on the opposition. Given that the Blues stuffed QPR 2-0 on the night in question, we'll presume the bloke in front went home without an unfeasibly hot, moistened pocket.

And you thought Liam Gallagher had always been a City fan.

The old monolithic East Stand before the recent facelift. Strange to think this inhospitable site is where excitable Japanese tourists now flock to take photos of each other. Note the advertised admission prices. In 1991 it cost £7 to stand and pay homage to the Blues, these days it'll set you back £22. Not that the football isn't more than three times better.

The gladiators enter the arena. As always, Kerry Dixon struts out fifth in line carrying the match ball - his pre-match superstition. Having notched 193 goals in his Chelsea career, he left the pitch carrying the match ball a few times too.

Chelsea thump Liverpool 4-2 - a cue for polite applause, manly backslapping, while children prepare to be passed overhead to the front. Was it really only 1991 and not 1891?

1991 and all that. An era when the only Italian name on the teamsheet was Dorigo. And this was what was meant by a hush-hush glamour signing - our Tony sneaking out to oblige the autograph hunters.

There's always one - the attention seeking terrace wag who can hear a camera shutter click from fully 70 yards. And what crowd scene would be complete without 'Radio 5' man (tucked behind our moustachioed friend's right arm) resplendent in anorak and headphones - a man who mistakenly believes that by intermittently tutting and uttering the words, 'United have scored again' he will instantly become the toast of the crowd.

The Old Bill take the Shed, 1991

"One day son, all this will be a hotel."

Tiers of joy. Jubilation in the East Stand as Chelsea salvage yet another improbable draw.

The West Stand in the days before it became an extension of the Groucho Club. In 1998 following the stand's demolition, it was possible to purchase one of these seats for your front room - a snip at £245.

A couple of unfamiliar objects in the home dressing room momentarily confuse Doug Rougvie.

The old press box, now since demolished. And not a modem in sight.

Fans seen at the Bridge when there were a lot more fashionable things to be done with your Saturday afternoons. The more cynical may note an absence of actors, pop stars and politicians amongst this lot.

Ah, the most precious and sought after square foot in the whole ground - the top corner. Blame a certain Mr Pat Nevin for the wear and tear.

Proof that it's not just the game that's been sanitised. Though if you'd been in
The Imperial for two hours before kick off, this was SW6's answer to paradise.

66

Back in 1991, the badge of faith was a thing to openly cherish - without fear of being reported for inciting a riot by a whinging Gooner.

A future season ticket holder gets the hang of things - turning her back on the game after only twenty minutes.

Tis the season to be melancholic. December 1991 and Man United fail to enter into the festive spirit of things, thumping the Blues 3-1. Leaving Chelsea fans with only cold turkey and a Boxing Day trip to Notts County to look forward to. And they lost that too.

A certain Man United striker comes in for some special attention. This was of course back in the days when Hughsie was widely reviled as a dirty, cheating, loathsome, soft permed, fat Manc. Now of course he's revered as a greying God (MBE). Funny what a change of shirt can do for your reputation.

1992 - and the directors' box stands to attention for the arrival of Mr Chelsea himself, chairman Ken Bates. The man who bought the club for £1 - inheriting debts of over £2 million in the process - may not be every fan's cup of Bovril but even those who baulked at his ambition to turn Chelsea into a vast leisure empire at least credit him with saving the ground and not selling Chelsea down the river.

Over the years, Chelsea have made wiping the floor with Spurs seem as perfunctory as washing the dishes. So predictable is 1992's 2-0 victory that one East Stand-er takes the opportunity to get his head down.

Faced with the banal offerings of club programmes and threatened by a sinister ID card scheme, the late eighties saw the birth of the football fans' own mouthpiece - the fanzine. The most regular of half a dozen Chelsea fanzines, and now in its tenth year, the Chelsea Independent still boasts 12,000 readers per issue, despite continued hostility from a certain bearded dairy farmer.

Say what you like about Bobby Campbell, but he wrote some riveting programme notes.

While the Shed had a fearsome reputation all of its own, the sartorial taste of some of its inhabitants also provoked widespread revulsion. The year is 1992 but the influence of Dexy's Midnight Runners still lingers like a bad smell.

He thinks it's all over...it wasn't. A jubilant Bill Clinton, (whose daughter of course is called Chelsea) gets to his feet to celebrate the Blues half time lead in the 1992 FA Cup quarter final tie against Sunderland. Predictably the Rokerites equalised and went on to win the replay 2-1. A result that 30,000 people later blamed entirely on the spectacularly foolish actions of one man.

The last game of the 1992 season and Chelsea fans stream triumphantly
onto the pitch to celebrate..er, the last game of the 1992 season.

The burger stall outside the Shed - and Suggs's secret Saturday job is revealed.

So rigidifyingly tedious are half-time intervals, fans willingly suffer a numb bum in order to read the enthralling reserve team match report (see left, right and top middle).

Love briefly blossoms at the Bridge. Two minutes after this photo was taken all notions of romance were curtailed when it slowly dawned on the young lady that what her boyfriend meant by tickets for a 'West End spectacular' was in fact this dreary mid table encounter against Coventry.

Talk about moving the goalposts. After promising the crowd a couple of goals, manager David Webb proves as good as his word.

The heavens herald the old West Stand complete with its footballing weather vane (left of floodlight). So that's how Jodi Morris served his apprenticeship. The vane has since become the subject of much speculation - rumours abound that it was unceremoniously dumped in a skip when the stand was demolished. Unless of course, you know better . . .

Chelsea outclass West Ham and Glenn Hoddle's introduction of blinding wing play forces some fans to don protective eyewear.

1994 Cup Final week in Wandsworth and plans for a street party are about to be put on hold for three years.

Cup Final day 1994. And by a strange quirk of coincidence, two hours later these happy shiny people all looked like the big fat blubbering baby behind them. Shame Umbro didn't have the guts to amend that poster to include, "Tillery, Wegerle, Rhodes Brown, Jones (V) . . ."

Predictably, come Cup Final week, business was brisk in the souvenir shop. Okay, so frilly panties were just about acceptable nighttime attire but goalkeeping gloves and a silk flag! What sort of sick mind would think about donning that combination come bedtime?

The winner of the competition to find the world's best replica of the FA Cup. Sadly he was the only person in a Chelsea shirt to lift a trophy that dismal afternoon.

Already looking a touch sick, imagine how this lot felt some ninety minutes later.

A date at Wembley is always an occasion worth dressing up for. Evidently this fan couldn't make up his mind whether to go as Jack Nicholson or a priest.

Wembley Way 1994 - and an excited Dani Behr contemplates her first live football match.

The aftermath of the 1994 Cup Final. Heads bowed against the pouring rain, a spanking by United all too fresh in the memory and yet the only talk is of Peacock's early effort that hit the bar - welcome to football's longest walk.

A highlight of children's birthday parties at the Bridge is always the pitch inspection. Though one world weary England international (back right) has already seen it all before.

Insert your own Dennis Wise caption.

The last pot Chelsea lifted prior to May '97. Given the difference in size between the home and away teapots, guess which one is Chelsea's.

Freshly ironed kit in the changing rooms. And what exactly is the point of putting branding on a jockstrap (centre)? Like thousands of people are going to see it are they? Not if Robert Fleck's wearing it they're not.

The mourning after. October 23rd 1996 and a young fan struggles to come to terms with news of Matthew Harding's death.

Within hours, the front gates of Stamford Bridge become a shrine to the man who, despite his enormous wealth, fans always regarded as one of their own.

Clutching scarves and mementos, fans queue to quietly pay their respects. Those who were at the Bridge that week can all pay testimony to the numbing silence that prevailed.

"The pleasure and the pain - Chelsea are both things to me. It's hard to explain, but like any great love, I don't question it or ever feel tempted to stray. I just know that Chelsea and I were meant for each other." Matthew Harding.

Given the amount of expletives uttered at the sight of this hastily written notice, who's to say the partially obscured sign in the background doesn't advise 'No Swearing'.

100

Window dressing in Battersea, Cup Final week, 1997. Oddly enough, this was virtually the shape of the real trophy after Wisey later rolled about on the turf with it.

Baker Street tube station, May 17th 1997 - Cup Final day. While the high spirited revellers give our photographer the finger, over the left shoulder of Buster Bloodvessel, something slightly more sinister is being pointed - the small but unmistakable shape of a pistol. What are the chances of seeing his ticket?

Wembley Way, May 1977. And excited youngsters succeed in putting names to their own faces. Though predictably not one of their heroes is English.

Anyone with the word AESLEHC imprinted on their cheek since the early eighties might recognise this fist.

Wem-ber-lee! Fans get an unexpected early view of the twin towers - courtesy of a decidedly blue version of Tango man.

The Blues Sisters strike a pose on Wembley Way. And you wondered what sort of person bought those fetching Chelsea lace knickers.

Outside the Fulham pub named after Doug Rougvie, a Chelsea fan celebrates the FA Cup win by donning a T-shirt emblazoned with a hideously disfigured Ruud Gullit. Nice.

'One man went to mow...' Though why he picked this moment, just seconds before the pitch was dug-up, remains a mystery. A perverse decision matched only by whoever was responsible for allowing the London Monarchs American football team to play at the Bridge during the '97 close season. It may have made commercial sense at the time but unfortunately all those shoulder pads, hard hats and ludicrous theatricals did nothing for the state of the pitch - forcing the turf to be hastily re-laid in August. Besides, isn't the pantomime season usually in December?

Ken Bates's vision begins to take shape as twelve acres of some of the most expensive real estate in south west London - known affectionately to some as Stamford Bridge - is slowly transformed into an area resembling Covent Garden.

Such is the gentrification of the game that even the notorious Shed now gets its own billing in glossy, plastic, light-up letters. Today's sanitised Shed End plays host to the new Chelsea Village Hotel - ad slogan; 'Come and have a go (at opening the minibar) if you think you're hard enough'.

The old West Stand ticket office displays a pronouncement echoed by thousands of die-hard supporters everywhere.

Tired of continually being asked for directions to the North Stand, one weary programme seller takes matters into his own hands.

Ever mindful to stop fans bringing alcohol into the ground, stewards can often be seen meticulously searching for hidden cans of Party Seven.

The home dugout after the 1-0 victory over Newcastle, 1997. Where once it would have been covered in well sucked fag ends and bits of gnawed fingernail, the only sign of a narrowly scraped victory now is a single blob of effortlessly chewed gum. That's how laid back the man Ruud is.

The press box 1997 style. 'Hold the back page - De Goey's just caught a corner'.

A new stand is erected where once the West Stand stood - and the ground is immediately transformed into something that would look more at home in the Dr Martens League. Who are this 'Else' lot anyway?

Thanks to the new Megastore and the wonders of digital technology, just £20 puts you in the frame alongside Wisey, the Duchess of Kent and some old tin pot.

The Megastore window. Insert your own Ken Bates caption.

Father and son get within touching distance of Chelsea's glittering prize. While son innocently remains under the illusion that this is the natural conclusion to every season, dad can hark back to the 26 years of fruitless hard labour that's gone before.

After inspiring the Blues to yet another home victory, Zola and his minder are mobbed by a crowd which includes two slightly puzzled Japanese tourists who believe they've stumbled across Al Pacino on a shopping trip down the King's Road. Not the sort of thing you could ever imagine happening to John Bumstead.